Grades 3-9

2/11/11

Ghosts

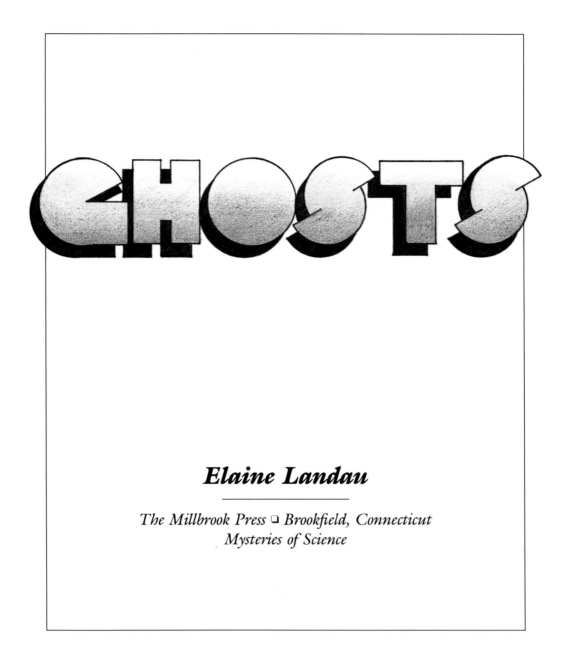

GHOSTS

Elaine Landau

The Millbrook Press ❑ Brookfield, Connecticut
Mysteries of Science

Photographs courtesy of North Wind Picture Archives: pp. 8,
11, 24; Bettmann Archive: pp. 15, 18; Photofest: pp. 21, 37;
AP/Wide World: p. 31; Skeptic Magazine, © Pat Linse: p. 34;
New York Public Library Picture Collection: p. 39.

Library of Congress Cataloging-in-Publication Data
Landau, Elaine.
Ghosts / Elaine Landau.
p.   cm.—(Mysteries of science)
Includes bibliographical references and index.
Summary: Recounts purportedly true stories involving ghosts,
poltergeists, and haunted houses and presents some of the theories
that have been advanced to explain these phenomena.
ISBN 1-56294-544-0 (Lib. bdg.)
1. Ghosts—Juvenile literature.   2. Poltergeists—Juvenile
literature.   3. Haunted houses—Juvenile literature.   [1. Ghosts.
2. Poltergeists.   3. Haunted houses.]   I. Title.   II. Series:
Landau, Elaine. Mysteries of science.
BF1461.L19   1995
133.1—dc20   95-18433   CIP   AC

Published by The Millbrook Press, Inc.
2 Old New Milford Road, Brookfield, Connecticut 06804

For Illana Harkavi

Contents

Chapter One
Ghosts 9

Chapter Two
Poltergeists! 17

Chapter Three
Haunted 23

Chapter Four
Fact or Fiction? 33

Notes 41
Glossary 43
Further Reading 44
Index 46

Ghosts

It happened at three o'clock in the morning
on a cold February day in 1962.

Richard, a teenager in Fairfield, Connecticut,
was suddenly awakened. From the corner of his eye
he noticed a strange light flooding the far side
of the room. It was then that he turned over and
saw the ghost. He described it in this way:
"She was a woman in white with long blond hair
and a glow around her."[1]

The graceful female smiled at the boy as she
glided across the room toward him. She did not
reply when he asked who she was, but only
floated out the window and into the darkness.

Richard did not tell anyone about his experience. He wondered if it had been a dream and doubted that he would be believed. However, one morning nearly six months later, his sister, greatly excited, ran down to the breakfast table, saying that she had seen a ghost in her room. She described a woman very much like the one Richard had seen, but she added—"She had a candle and floated back and forth from the closet to the bed."[2] When the family went upstairs to where his sister said the ghost had stood, they were startled by what they saw. Dripped across the hardwood floor was candle wax.

❏ ❏ ❏

Although this "Yankee" ghost appeared in New England, tales of spirits or the restless dead are common throughout the United States. In the mid-1960s, ghost sightings of a mother and child who had died in a fire in Indiana captured public attention. People from around the country flocked to the state, hoping to catch a glimpse of the spirit pair, who were said to leave scratch marks on car windows. The ongoing interest continued for some time despite rumors that the story was just a hoax invented by some college students.

What makes the thought of ghosts walking among us so fascinating to many people? Is it simply part of a universal need to believe that there is life after death? Or is the pain of losing a loved one eased by thinking that he or she still exists in some form?

Ghosts have been appearing for centuries, at least
in literature. In William Shakespeare's play Hamlet,
the ghost of Hamlet's father appears to him.

For thousands of years the notion of spirits who return from beyond the grave has played an important role in the history and religion of cultures around the world. Many civilizations have adopted the idea of a special resting place for the dead. Ghosts have often been described as spirits who were somehow blocked from reaching this final destination.

A spirit might be destined to roam the earth for a number of reasons. Some are thought to be the ghosts of people who had been brutally murdered. When sighted, they might repeatedly reenact their murder or another unfortunate event in their lives. Some people believe that these spirits cannot rest until their deaths are avenged.

Other ghosts thought doomed to wander are those whose bodies were either left unburied or buried without a religious service or headstone marker. Ghosts whose buried bodies have been disturbed are sometimes thought to join the ranks of the restless dead as well.

Some ghosts are believed to be those who were guilty of genuine evil or serious misconduct while alive. Unable to rest in peace, such spirits are frequently described as moaning, groaning, or dragging their chains. Still others are believed to be the spirits of people who died before completing an important task. These ghosts supposedly remain to finish what was begun or to warn loved ones of impending danger.

That is what happened one night when a woman and her daughter were driving home along a dark, winding country road. Suddenly the woman's recently deceased husband appeared several yards ahead of their car. He raised his hand as if to warn them not to drive on. Although they hurried over to where they had seen him, he had vanished by the time they arrived. From the place where he had appeared, however, the mother and daughter could see that the bridge they had been about to cross had been washed out by a recent storm. Both feel certain that they would have been killed if he had not warned them.

There are also numerous accounts of a person's ghost coming to a loved one before leaving this world. One such well-known case involved a British woman who was living in India in 1917. As she walked into her living room one day, she was startled to see her half-brother standing there smiling at her. World War I was being waged at the time, and she thought he was on active duty with England's Royal Flying Corps. When his image faded away seconds later, she realized that he had not come to see her while on leave. She later learned that the incident occurred at the precise time of her brother's death, just after his plane was shot down on a bombing mission.

❑ ❑ ❑

In the cases described here, ghosts appeared to their loved ones in familiar, well-defined forms. Other stories of ghostly encounters, however, differ. Some people claim merely to sense the presence of a ghost around them. They may feel a chill when there is no open door or window nearby, or they may experience an eerie feeling they find difficult to describe.

One junior high school science teacher could not understand why he suddenly felt cold on an unusually hot day while conducting a summer school class. The chill lasted several minutes, causing him to put back on the suit jacket he had removed earlier. Upon returning home that day he received a call informing him that his twin brother had been killed in a boating accident more than a thousand miles away.

At times even those who doubt that ghosts exist have changed their minds following an unnerving occurrence. That's what happened to Glenn, a local fireman on duty the night an unusual emergency call came into the firehouse. Some transformers had blown up near a cemetery. Glenn took off for the site, bringing a police officer along in the truck with him. As they approached the cemetery Glenn heard the officer yell, "Look out!" Squarely in the truck's path stood a slender woman dressed in white. Glenn slammed on the brakes to avoid hitting her, but it was too late.

The thrust of the truck threw the woman over its hood before she fell back to the ground. When Glenn stepped out of the vehicle, however, the woman was nowhere in sight. Although he and the police officer were certain she had been struck, both claimed that "no body, no blood, no clothing"

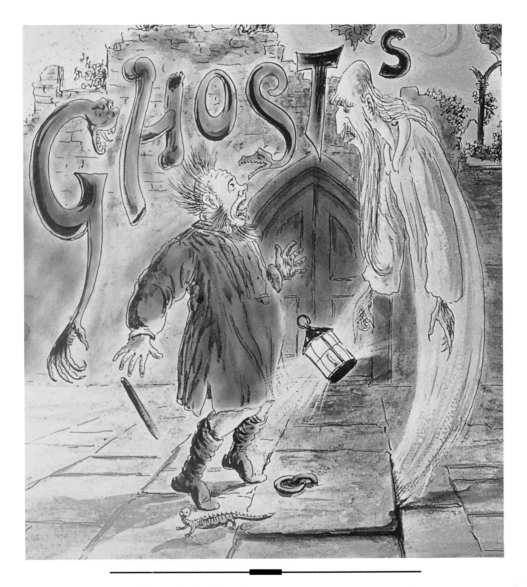

In this typical ghost/human encounter, a man is terrified by a ghost that rises up out of a crypt.

could be found. At first Glenn did not believe what had happened. But after contacting the local police department and three local hospitals, he learned that "nobody reported any missing persons, hit and runs, nothing."[3]

A psychic investigator looked into this incident and similar ones near the same location. Attempting to capture on film what Glenn had seen, the investigator turned to psychic photography. In psychic photography the person holding the camera supposedly does not actually photograph the ghost. Instead, ghosts are thought to imprint their own image onto the film by taking the energy to do so from living things around them. The psychic investigator photographed the graveyard site under varied weather conditions and when the pictures were developed, a number of people claimed to plainly see the figure of a woman.

Did the investigator capture an image of the woman in white thought to have stepped in front of Glenn's vehicle? Do ghosts exist, or have they merely been invented by people with overactive imaginations? These answers may not always be as clear-cut as some would like.

Poltergeists!

Poltergeists! These "noisy spirits" are often described as annoying or tricky ghosts that are never seen but often heard.

Poltergeists are thought to be responsible for making repeated rapping or knocking sounds, tossing objects about (regardless of their size or weight), lifting and moving furniture, and continually turning lights on and off.

Invisible poltergeists are also frequently blamed for ringing church bells, playing pianos, organs or other instruments, and sending echoing bursts of laughter through houses or other buildings.

One woman, who felt she was the victim of a poltergeist, described her experience as follows: "It started on the first night in the house. [It] began with walking around, cupboard doors open and shutting. . . . It got to a point where we could hear a man behind us laughing, and we'd turn around and no one would be there. He grabbed me on the shoulder and spun me physically around and no one was behind me."[1] Even after the woman moved, the poltergeist and its unnerving antics seemed to follow her.

❑ ❑ ❑

Reports of poltergeist outbreaks from various parts of the world date back hundreds of years. Often these episodes have been attributed to mischievous spirits. In earlier times, little objective evidence was collected to support this theory. And unfortunately, poltergeist activity is especially difficult to investigate, since it generally continues for only a limited time.

If, after a few days or weeks, the people involved call for outside aid, there is often little left to see. This means

Spiritualistic experimentation can have some surprising results. Levitating furniture is a common occurrence in a household that has a resident poltergeist.

that an investigator must depend on the testimony of witnesses. When all the witnesses either are family members or live together, investigators may seek out other sources. At times, the members of a family have acted together to put over a hoax. In other cases, family members may try to protect a disturbed relative they suspect has either greatly exaggerated or lied.

There are, however, instances of poltergeist activity involving numerous witnesses who did not know one another. A famous example, known as the Sauchie Poltergeist, occurred in Scotland in 1960 and centered on an intelligent, outgoing eleven-year-old girl named Virginia. The problem started on the evening of November 22, when a noise that sounded like a bouncing ball was heard coming from Virginia's room. As the girl came downstairs to complain about the commotion, the noise followed her.

Other strange things began to happen as well. It soon became clear that the poltergeist was not content to just remain at home. Before long, disruptive things started to happen in Virginia's classroom. Once, when Virginia stood next to the blackboard, the pointer resting on the rim of the board shook and fell off. The desk behind Virginia also rose more than an inch (2.5 centimeters) off the ground before settling back down.

A running tape recorder at Virginia's house continued to pick up a wide range of sounds, including loud raps, knocks, and slams. A few weeks later the occurrences

The movie "Poltergeist" brought to life the terror some say is caused by these active, sometimes playful, sometimes violent, spirits.

stopped completely. Despite a careful review of the case by psychic investigators, however, no one was certain precisely what had occurred or why it had stopped.

❏ ❏ ❏

There are, nevertheless, certain recognizable characteristics of what is often labeled a poltergeist outbreak. Most published cases include reports of a variety of loud sounds repeated over a period of time. Poltergeist activity is as likely to take place in broad daylight as at night. Most poltergeist reports also center on an individual rather than a particular place or building. The vast majority of poltergeist incidents involve females. A study of these cases has shown that women are twice as likely as men to be the focus. Adolescent girls are most frequently affected—an overwhelming number of outbreaks involve females between ten and twenty years old.

Haunted

In the Lower Garden District of New Orleans
stands a spacious home built in the 1800s.
Although the dwelling is an elegant reminder
of the Old South, it has remained unoccupied
most of the time. That is because, some say,
the house is haunted.

The trouble is supposed to have begun some-
time between 1860 and 1870. The housekeeper,
a pretty teenager thought to be the owner's
distant cousin, became pregnant. Although no one
was certain who the baby's father was, it was
rumored to be the married master of the house.

In any case, the baby did not remain in the
upstairs nursery very long.

There are many legends of long-dead people reappearing as ghosts. Some believe they can be conjured up by the concentrated efforts of people gathered together for a séance.

It had been born deformed, and the family wanted nothing to do with the child and was relieved when it died shortly after its birth. To this day, however, no one can say whether the baby's death was due to natural causes or to murder.

Since the family did not want anyone to know about the child, the infant was buried within the nursery walls.

Soon afterward, its young mother became ill with yellow fever and died as well.

The family soon realized it would not so easily be rid of the girl who had threatened its good name with scandal. Tormented by her baby's untimely death, the young woman's spirit supposedly could not rest. Witnesses swear that her ghost walks the halls of this once stately home. Some say she roams the house to "protect" her baby—a task she failed at while alive.

According to legend, her ghost was once seen at a dinner party given more than one hundred years after her death. Guests were said to have looked on in amazement as the ghost of a young girl with blue eyes and long brown hair appeared before them. She wore a bluish-green Mardi Gras ballgown, which the new residents claimed looked very much like a dress they had found crumpled in a musty closet of the house.

But perhaps the most unsettling area of the house was the nursery where the infant was buried more than a century ago.

When the house was renovated, the wallpaper was stripped from the nursery walls. To the residents' surprise, a large black patch about 2 feet (0.5 meters) wide and 6 feet (almost 2 meters) long was found on the wall. They tried to paint over it, but the dark color kept showing through. As one painter put it, "I guess we used ten to twelve coats before it looked halfway decent."[1]

To completely hide the discolored wall area, a large painting was hung over it. But it did not stay up very long. One evening a loud crash was heard coming from the room. Upon investigation, the painting and its frame were found shattered on the floor some distance from where it had hung. It looked as though someone had torn it off the wall and thrown it across the room.

Thinking that vibrations from the outside traffic had caused the painting to fall, the residents replaced it. This time they covered the whole wall with an assortment of paintings. But the new artwork was up for only a short time before the household was awakened during the night by a "tremendous crash." Large as well as small pictures were found tossed on the nursery floor, as were a number of porcelain figurines and several lamps. Perhaps the most disturbing aspect of what had occurred were the gouge marks left in the wall where someone or something "had physically pulled everything [the pictures] out."[2]

❏ ❏ ❏

Old private homes are not the only supposedly haunted dwellings. Inns, castles, museums, factories, and even nightclubs have been said to have their share of ghosts.

One nightspot supposedly haunted by several ghosts is Bobby Mackey's Music World in Wilder, Kentucky. Janet Mackey, the owner's wife, claims to have had a few dangerous encounters with these spirits. She first felt something strange when she and her husband looked at the property before purchasing it. While they were walking through the building, a door opened by itself. Janet Mackey also thought she heard voices when no was there.

But that was just the beginning. When she was five and a half months pregnant she was pushed down a flight of stairs at the club by what she feels was "a spirit, demon, or something."

Similar experiences were fairly common among the nightclub's staff and customers. Mary Torres, an employee at Bobby Mackey's Music World, said she was in one of the stockrooms when an indescribable force angrily shoved her up against the wall and a voice told her to get out. Some customers as well as employees said that at different times they had seen a headless girl floating through the establishment. Still others reported seeing the ghost of a dark-haired man with a handlebar mustache. Several people had even heard the jukebox play the song "Anniversary Waltz" on its own.

Among those who may have experienced the supernatural at Bobby Mackey's Music World was law enforcement officer Lieutenant Steve Seiter. Seiter was called on to help when a serious auto accident occurred in front of the nightclub. Seven people were involved, two of whom were killed. While assisting the victims before the ambulance arrived, the officer was approached by a woman dressed in white whom he thought worked at the nightclub. Handing Lieutenant

Seiter some red-and-white checkered tablecloths, she asked, "Will these help you?"[3] Grateful for the aid, he used them to cover the injured victims.

The following day Seiter called Bobby Mackey to thank him for sending the tablecloths. He was shocked to learn that no one on Mackey's staff matched the description of the helpful woman. In fact, Mackey did not even own any red-and-white checkered tablecloths.

The persistent reports of ghosts at Bobby Mackey's Music World led to an investigation of the premises' history. As it turned out, the building and grounds had an extremely violent past. In the early 1800s, a slaughterhouse occupied the site. The slaughtered animals and their drained blood attracted a cult of satanic worshipers who frequently conducted their secret rituals after dark on the grounds.

Besides the animal slaughter, several people had been killed near the club. Among these was Pearl Bryan, a young woman whose headless body was found in 1896 about 2½ miles (4 kilometers) from the building that later housed Bobby Mackey's nightclub. Despite an extensive search of the surrounding area, the woman's head was never recovered.

Two men, Alfonzo Walling and Scott Jackson, were charged with the crime. As both were dental students, some think they beheaded the girl so that her decomposed body could not be identified through dental records. But to their dismay she was found shortly after the murder, and was further judged to be five and a half months pregnant at the time. Scott Jackson was believed to be the father of her unborn child. It was thought that he and his good friend killed her so that Jackson would not have to marry her.

Walling and Jackson were found guilty and sentenced to be hanged. But they did not go peacefully to their graves. While standing with the rope around his neck, Alfonzo Walling proclaimed his innocence one last time. "I did not partake in the murder," he told the officials and spectators present. "I knew of the murder, but I was not involved in it, and if you hang me, I will come back here and haunt this area ever after."[4]

Some think that is how the haunting of Bobby Mackey's Music World began. Newspaper accounts of the time reveal that Walling's threat was swiftly felt. Soon after the hanging, the trial judge was crippled as the result of a serious injury, and one of the prosecution's lawyers was murdered months later.

As time passed Bobby Mackey's Music World was the site of still more brutality. Believing that several other ghosts may also occupy the premises, a psychic visited Bobby Mackey's Music World. Some think she may have seen the ghosts of Pearl Bryan and Scott Jackson, among others. The psychic described her experience: "I went into one room, and there was a woman, a ghost, sitting there and she was holding her head, like this, and all she kept saying was, 'Oh, my head. Oh, my head'. And then there was a man standing next to her saying, just yelling at her, over and over and saying, 'It's your fault we're here.' "[5]

❏ ❏ ❏

If ghosts are causing the problems at Bobby Mackey's Music World, the case would probably not be beyond the scope of "ghostbusters" Ed and Lorraine Warren. As directors of the New England Society for Psychic Research, the couple has been asked to investigate countless seemingly unnatural occurrences. Through the years they have also worked closely with the clergy of many faiths to dispel demons from various dwellings.

The Warrens not only feel that ghosts exist but that these unworldly beings can sometimes harm the living. "We have numerous cases of people [who] have been picked up, thrown against the walls," Ed Warren noted. He continued, "We're talking about film recordings, credible people and organizations involved here. We're not talking about Hollywood hype."[6]

Ian Currie, formerly a university sociology professor, has a special interest in dehaunting houses. Currie feels that ghosts are lingering spirits who simply refuse to accept the fact that they are dead and are often hesitant to leave familiar surroundings. "I tell them [the ghosts] they're dead—they usually give me an argument," Currie explained. "Forty percent of ghosts have unfinished business—they won't rest until it's communicated."[7]

Ed and Lorraine Warren (right) are two of
many real-life "ghostbusters" who believe that spirits
are among us. Here they are pictured with a client.

Ghostbuster Echo Bodine stresses that her work is more like ghost counseling than ghostbusting. Bodine describes how it works: "We go in. We ask them first of all, what their name is, why they're there, and then we talk them into the other side, which is commonly referred to as heaven."[8]

Though Bodine visited Bobby Mackey's Music World hoping to improve the situation, she warns that ghost counseling is not always effective. She said, "We have free will in death as well as in life, and so, sometimes they just choose— no I'm not going."[9]

If that is so, some think the disturbances at Bobby Mackey's Music World may go on indefinitely.

Fact or Fiction?

Do you believe in ghosts? If you do, you are not alone. According to a national Gallup poll, one in ten Americans claims to have either seen or been in the presence of a ghost (heard, smelled, or felt it).

Yet others seriously doubt this. They feel that an examination of such incidents will reveal other causes.

"I don't think there's a ghost of a chance of these things really being real," warned Dr. Michael Shermer, publisher of *Skeptic* magazine and a professor at Occidental College. "There's a number of explanations. First of all, you have normal physical phenomena. My house was haunted with strange rapping sounds and clawing noises in the basement. I didn't call a ghostbuster. It was rats."[1]

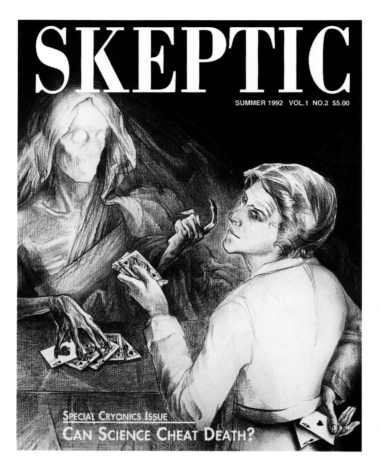

SKEPTIC

SUMMER 1992 VOL.1 NO.2 $5.00

SPECIAL CRYONICS ISSUE
CAN SCIENCE CHEAT DEATH?

Skeptic is a magazine "Devoted to the Investigation and Promotion of Science and Rational Skepticism." In other words, they don't believe in ghosts.

In some instances, weather, lighting conditions, the time of day, or a number of other circumstances can influence what a person sees or hears. Dr. Shermer described what occurs: "These things usually happen at night or when it's cooler. The air is denser, so sound travels farther. I can hear noises from my next-door neighbor's house for example. If my window is open it sounds like children playing in the next room and they're not. It's the next-door neighbors."[2]

Psychologist Robert Baker, formerly with the University of Kentucky, believes that a state known as hypnopompic sleep may also be responsible for people thinking they have seen ghosts. During hypnopompic sleep, which occurs as someone awakens, a person may experience a dreamlike vision, or so-called waking dream. Although the person is still partly asleep, he or she may feel fully awake and be certain that a ghost has appeared in the room.

There is also the theory that people's expectations influence what they see. That may be why ghost stories are often so similar.

Certain images—that of a woman dressed in white, an eighteenth-century horse-drawn carriage, or a ghost dragging his chains—have been passed along through the years. Therefore, if people visiting a supposedly haunted castle hear a sudden noise they may tend to think it is a ghost rather than a cat knocking over an ashtray or lamp.

Other ghost sightings have proven to be hoaxes. For example, in 1976 two researchers in parapsychology (the science dealing with occurrences that cannot be explained in terms of our present knowledge) were contacted by a man from Long Island, New York, who told them that his house was haunted. The man said the haunting was probably connected to a mass murder that had occurred there two years before.

One of the researchers visited New York and met the man and his family. In discussing the now imprisoned mass murderer, the man living in the house showed the researcher a sample of the killer's handwriting. To the investigator's surprise, the signature was on a contract for the book and film rights to a ghost story! Since the parapsychologists had no evidence of a haunting besides the man's story, they felt he might be more interested in sharing the killer's profits than sharing the truth.

Others, however, were readily fooled. Before long a best-selling book and movie, *The Amityville Horror,* were based on the tale. Later, an attorney representing the murderer's family exposed the story as a hoax devised by his clients and the family that had moved into the house. Claiming that they had not received their full share of the profits, the murderer's family was suing the others.

❏ ❏ ❏

After weeding out the hoaxes, parapsychologists have tried to classify different types of ghost sightings. In cases where a ghost is seen by just one individual, some parapsychologists think that the deceased's spirit may have telepathically (through thoughts, not words) reached out to that person and so created the hallucination of a "ghost."

In situations where a number of people see the same ghost over a period of time, researchers suggest a different explanation. They think that "super ESP" may be responsible in these cases. ESP stands for extrasensory perception, and super ESP is psychic ability at a greater level and sensitivity than is generally studied in laboratories. Parapsychologists who advance this theory believe that at times a horrendous past event leaves its imprint on a particular location. Later on, particularly sensitive visitors to the site somehow psychically obtain the story.

The movie The Amityville Horror, *supposedly based on a true story, made a terrifying spectacle. In real life, it turned out to be a hoax.*

Yet other parapsychologists disagree. They argue that ghost sightings are not images of past violence but are caused by the surviving spirit or soul of the dead person. This theory is based on the belief that some part of a human being exists after death.

Parapsychologists have also distinguished between ghost sightings and poltergeist outbreaks. Generally, in ghost sightings the spirit engages in the same behavior (such as pacing back and forth) each time it appears. It rarely interacts with onlookers regardless of who is present.

Though poltergeist outbreaks were once thought to be caused by mischievous or even malicious spirits, parapsychologists no longer believe this. They have learned that the problem is actually caused by the living person on whom these outbreaks tend to focus.

In the vast majority of cases, that individual is an adolescent female experiencing some degree of psychological (mental) stress. Researchers think that the energy produced by this stress is somehow used for psychokinesis—the ability to move objects without touching them. Therefore, although the person involved may not be aware of it, he or she is actually responsible for rearranging pieces of furniture, opening and closing doors, or making dishes fall from the table to the floor.

But countless adolescents have weathered stress-filled periods without poltergeist outbreaks. What then is different about the relatively few young people who become the

A CORNISH LITANY.

FROM GHOULIES AND GHOSTIES AND LONG LEGGITY BEASTIES AND THINGS THAT GO BUMP IN THE NIGHT GOOD LORD DELIVER US

People have differing opinions on the existence of ghosts. But a good ghost story seems to give everyone a few goose bumps.

focus of this activity? Clues to the answer may be found in recent brain research. In a survey of ninety-two of these young people, nearly 25 percent had experienced mild seizures, trancelike states, or similar brain disorders.[3] Though significantly more research in this area is needed, it has been suggested that there may be a link between psychokinesis and seizurelike disturbances in the brain.

Unfortunately, in dealing with a subject such as poltergeists or ghosts, there are few hard and fast answers. The search for truth is further complicated by the fact that only a handful of serious scientists are willing to explore this realm. That is because such investigations frequently require a good deal of time and funding, without providing solid scientific evidence. Even when the investigator carefully documents events through the testimony of reliable witnesses and audio or film recordings, these studies are often not taken seriously. As a result, scientific as well as public understanding of these incidents has barely advanced through the years.

Some still argue that just because these cases are not readily investigated, does not mean that hauntings have not occurred. In response, their critics stress that no such claim has ever been proven beyond a doubt. That leaves us with the challenging question that has been asked throughout the years. Are ghosts and hauntings simply a part of our folklore? Or do they fall into an area that science still does not fully understand? We must all decide for ourselves.

Notes

Chapter One

1. Richard Barnes, "One Chilling Midwinter Night," *Yankee* (January 1993), p. 24.
2. Ibid.
3. Sally Jessy Raphael, "I Was Haunted & Terrorized," Transcript #1603 (October 28, 1994).

Chapter Two

1. Sally Jessy Raphael, "I Was Haunted & Terrorized," Transcript #1603 (October 28, 1994).

Chapter Three

1. Michael Swindle, "A Ghost Story," *New Orleans* (May 1989), p. 91.
2. Ibid., p. 92.
3. Sally Jessy Raphael, "I Believe in Ghosts," Transcript #1526 (July 13, 1994).

4. Ibid.
5. Ibid.
6. Ibid.
7. Joyce and Richard Wolkomir, "Ghostbusters at Work," *McCall's* (July 1989), p. 106.
8. Sally Jessy Raphael, "I Was Haunted & Terrorized," Transcript #1603 (October 28, 1994).
9: Ibid.

Chapter Four

1. Sally Jessy Raphael, "I Believe in Ghosts," Transcript #1526 (July 13, 1994).
2. Ibid.
3. Richard S. Broughton, Ph.D., *Parapsychology: The Controversial Science* (New York: Ballantine Books, 1991), p. 232.

Glossary

ESP (extrasensory perception)—knowing about an object, thought, or event without having seen, heard, or read about it

hallucination—seeing or hearing something that is not there

hypnopompic sleep—the state just before waking, in which dreamlike visions can occur and be mistaken for real events

Mardi Gras—a carnival celebrated in certain cities

parapsychology—the study of occurrences that cannot be explained in terms of present knowledge or scientific theory

poltergeist—a mischievous ghost or force thought by some to be responsible for causing loud noises, moving or breaking objects, and other similar activities

psychokinesis—the ability to move an object without touching it

ritual—any regularly performed act or custom

spirit—a being without a physical body; of or relating to such beings

Further Reading

Aylesworth, Thomas G. *Vampires and Other Ghosts.* Reading, Massachusetts: Addison-Wesley, 1972.

Ballinger, Erich. *Monster Manual: A Complete Guide to Your Favorite Creatures.* Minneapolis: Lerner, 1994.

Brown, Roberta Simpson. *The Queen of the Cold-Blooded Tales.* Little Rock: August House, 1993.

Cohen, Daniel. *Ghosts of the Deep.* New York: Putnam, 1993.

———. *The Ghosts of War.* New York: Putnam, 1990.

———. *Young Ghosts.* New York: Cobblehill, 1994.

Hamilton, Virginia. *The Dark Way: Stories from the Spirit World.* New York: HBJ/Gulliver, 1990.

Haskins, James. *The Headless Haunt and Other African-American Ghost Stories.* New York: HarperCollins, 1994.

Raw Head, Bloody Bones: African American Tales of the Supernatural. Comp. by Mary E. Lyons. New York: Scribner's, 1991.

Schwartz, Alvin. *Scary Stories to Tell in the Dark.* New York: HarperCollins, 1981.

Why Am I Grown So Cold? Poems of the Unknowable. Ed. by Myra Cohn Livingston. New York: Macmillan/Margaret K. McElderry, 1982.

Young, Richard, and Young, Judy Dockrey. *The Scary Story Reader.* Little Rock: August House, 1993.

Index

Page numbers in *italics* refer to illustrations.

Adolescent females, 22, 38
Amityville Horror, The (movie), 36, *37*

Baker, Robert, 35
Bobby Mackey's Music World, Wilder, Kentucky, 26-30, 32
Bodine, Echo, 32
Brain research, 40
Bryan, Pearl, 28, 29

Clergy, 30
Currie, Ian, 30

ESP (extrasensory perception), 36-37

Fairfield, Connecticut, 9-10

Ghostbusters, 30, *31,* 32
Ghost sightings, 9-10, 12-14, 16, 27, 29-30, 35, 36, 38

Hallucination, 36
Hamlet (Shakespeare), *11*
Haunted houses, 23-27, 35-36
Hoaxes, 10, 20, 35-36
Hypnopompic sleep, 35

India, 13

Indiana, 10

Jackson, Scott, 28-29

Levitation, *18*
Long Island, New York, 35-36

Mackey, Bobby, 27, 28
Mackey, Janet, 26-27
Mardi Gras, 25

New England Society for Psychic
  Research, 30
New Orleans, Louisiana, 23-26

Parapsychology, 35-38
Poltergeist (movie), *21*
Poltergeists, 17, *18*, 19-20, *21*, 22,
  38
Psychic photography, 16

Psychokinesis, 38-39

Sauchie Poltergeist, 20
Scotland, 20
Seance, *24*
Seiter, Steve, 27-28
Shakespeare, William, *11*
Shermer, Michael, 33, 34
Skeptic magazine, 33, *34*
Spirits, 12
Super ESP (extrasensory percep-
  tion), 36-37

Torres, Mary, 27

Waking dream, 35
Walling, Alonzo, 28-29
Warren, Ed, 30, *31*
Warren, Lorraine, 30, *31*

"Yankee" ghost, 9-10

About the Author

Elaine Landau received her bachelor's degree from New York University in English and journalism and her master's degree in library and information science from Pratt Institute.

She has worked as a newspaper reporter, editor, and youth services librarian, and has especially enjoyed writing more than 85 books for young people.

Ms. Landau lives in New Jersey.